50 Sizzle and Spice Dishes

By: Kelly Johnson

Table of Contents

- Spicy Cajun Chicken Skillet
- Thai Red Curry Shrimp
- Chipotle Beef Fajitas
- Szechuan Stir-Fry Vegetables
- Habanero BBQ Ribs
- Jamaican Jerk Chicken
- Korean Spicy Bulgogi Beef
- Peri-Peri Grilled Chicken
- Spicy Shrimp Tacos with Lime Crema
- Hot and Sour Soup
- Ghost Pepper Chicken Wings
- Blackened Fish Tacos
- Spicy Chorizo Stuffed Peppers
- Firecracker Shrimp
- Tandoori Chicken
- Spicy Beef Empanadas
- Spicy Lamb Koftas

- Harissa Chicken Thighs
- Sweet and Spicy Korean Fried Chicken
- Mango Habanero Pork Tenderloin
- Sichuan Spicy Noodles
- Chili Garlic Shrimp
- Cajun Crawfish Etouffee
- Peri-Peri Prawns
- Spicy Pork Bulgogi
- Chili Lime Grilled Steak
- Thai Basil Beef
- Baked Buffalo Cauliflower Wings
- Fiery Chipotle Mac and Cheese
- Spicy Stuffed Chicken Breast
- Sizzling Beef Stir Fry
- Korean Spicy Pork Belly
- Sweet and Spicy Hot Wings
- Spicy Indian Butter Chicken
- Chipotle Black Bean Tacos
- Fire-Grilled Sriracha Steak

- Sizzling Shrimp and Vegetables
- Spicy Korean Kimchi Pancakes
- Spicy Cajun Pasta
- Spicy Cilantro Lime Chicken
- Fiery Garlic Chili Chicken
- Chili Mango Fish Tacos
- Hot Pepper Jack Grilled Cheese
- Roasted Jalapeño Popper Chicken
- Sriracha Honey Grilled Salmon
- Spicy Tofu Stir Fry
- Spicy Marinated Lamb Chops
- Fire-Roasted Salsa and Grilled Chicken
- Thai Green Curry with Vegetables
- Spicy Chipotle Salmon

Spicy Cajun Chicken Skillet

- Ingredients:

    1. 4 chicken breasts
    2. 2 tbsp Cajun seasoning
    3. 1 tsp smoked paprika
    4. 1/2 tsp garlic powder
    5. 1 tbsp olive oil
    6. 1/2 cup bell peppers, sliced
    7. 1/2 cup onions, sliced
    8. 1/4 cup chicken broth
    9. Salt and pepper to taste

- Instructions:

    1. Coat the chicken with Cajun seasoning, paprika, garlic powder, salt, and pepper.
    2. Heat olive oil in a skillet over medium heat. Add chicken and cook for 6-7 minutes per side until golden and cooked through.
    3. Add sliced bell peppers and onions, and sauté for 3-4 minutes until tender.
    4. Pour in chicken broth, stirring to deglaze the pan. Let it simmer for a couple of minutes.
    5. Serve with a side of rice or over a bed of greens.

Thai Red Curry Shrimp

- Ingredients:

    1. 1 lb shrimp, peeled and deveined
    2. 2 tbsp red curry paste
    3. 1 can coconut milk
    4. 1 tbsp fish sauce
    5. 1 tbsp brown sugar
    6. 1/2 cup bell peppers, sliced
    7. 1/2 cup onions, sliced
    8. Fresh basil leaves
    9. 1 tbsp olive oil

- Instructions:

    1. Heat olive oil in a large pan over medium heat. Add shrimp and cook for 2-3 minutes on each side. Set aside.
    2. In the same pan, add red curry paste and cook for 1 minute.
    3. Add coconut milk, fish sauce, and brown sugar. Stir to combine and bring to a simmer.
    4. Add bell peppers, onions, and shrimp back into the pan. Cook for an additional 5 minutes, allowing the sauce to thicken.
    5. Garnish with fresh basil and serve with steamed jasmine rice.

Chipotle Beef Fajitas

- Ingredients:

    1. 1 lb flank steak, sliced thin
    2. 2 tbsp chipotle in adobo sauce, minced
    3. 1 tsp cumin
    4. 1 tsp garlic powder
    5. 1 tbsp lime juice
    6. 1 tbsp olive oil
    7. 1/2 cup bell peppers, sliced
    8. 1/2 cup onions, sliced
    9. Warm tortillas

- Instructions:

    1. Marinate the beef with chipotle in adobo, cumin, garlic powder, lime juice, and olive oil for at least 30 minutes.
    2. Heat a pan over medium-high heat and cook the beef strips for 3-4 minutes until browned and cooked through.
    3. Remove the beef and sauté bell peppers and onions in the same pan for 5-6 minutes.
    4. Serve the beef and veggies in warm tortillas with your favorite toppings.

Szechuan Stir-Fry Vegetables

- Ingredients:

    1. 1 cup broccoli florets
    2. 1/2 cup carrots, julienned
    3. 1/2 cup snap peas
    4. 2 tbsp soy sauce
    5. 1 tbsp rice vinegar
    6. 1 tbsp chili paste
    7. 1 tbsp sesame oil
    8. 1 tsp Szechuan peppercorns
    9. 2 cloves garlic, minced
    10. 1/4 cup green onions, chopped

- Instructions:

    1. Heat sesame oil in a wok over medium-high heat. Add garlic and Szechuan peppercorns, sautéing for 1-2 minutes.
    2. Add carrots, snap peas, and broccoli, stir-frying for 5-6 minutes.
    3. Stir in soy sauce, rice vinegar, and chili paste, cooking for an additional 2 minutes.
    4. Garnish with green onions and serve with steamed rice or noodles.

Habanero BBQ Ribs

- Ingredients:
    1. 1 rack of baby back ribs
    2. 2 tbsp brown sugar
    3. 1 tbsp paprika
    4. 1 tbsp garlic powder
    5. 1 tsp cayenne pepper
    6. 2 habanero peppers, finely chopped
    7. 1 cup BBQ sauce
    8. Salt and pepper to taste

- Instructions:
    1. Preheat the oven to 300°F (150°C).
    2. Mix brown sugar, paprika, garlic powder, cayenne, salt, and pepper. Rub the mixture generously on the ribs.
    3. Wrap ribs in foil and bake for 2.5 hours.
    4. In a saucepan, combine BBQ sauce and habaneros, simmering for 5 minutes.
    5. Brush the sauce onto the ribs and grill for an additional 10-15 minutes until caramelized.

Jamaican Jerk Chicken

- Ingredients:

    1. 4 chicken thighs
    2. 2 tbsp allspice
    3. 1 scotch bonnet pepper, minced
    4. 1 tbsp thyme
    5. 2 tbsp soy sauce
    6. 1 tbsp lime juice
    7. 1 tsp cinnamon
    8. Salt and pepper to taste

- Instructions:

    1. Mix allspice, scotch bonnet pepper, thyme, soy sauce, lime juice, cinnamon, salt, and pepper in a bowl.
    2. Coat the chicken with the marinade and let it sit for at least 2 hours.
    3. Grill the chicken for 5-7 minutes on each side until cooked through.
    4. Serve with rice and beans.

Korean Spicy Bulgogi Beef

- Ingredients:

    1. 1 lb thinly sliced beef
    2. 2 tbsp soy sauce
    3. 1 tbsp gochujang (Korean chili paste)
    4. 1 tbsp brown sugar
    5. 2 cloves garlic, minced
    6. 1 tbsp sesame oil
    7. 1/4 cup green onions, chopped

- Instructions:

    1. Mix soy sauce, gochujang, brown sugar, garlic, and sesame oil in a bowl.
    2. Marinate the beef for 30 minutes.
    3. Heat a pan over medium-high heat and cook the beef for 2-3 minutes until browned.
    4. Garnish with green onions and serve with steamed rice.

Peri-Peri Grilled Chicken

- Ingredients:
    1. 4 chicken breasts
    2. 2 tbsp peri-peri sauce
    3. 1 tbsp olive oil
    4. 1 tbsp lime juice
    5. 1 tsp garlic powder
    6. Salt and pepper to taste

- Instructions:
    1. Mix peri-peri sauce, olive oil, lime juice, garlic powder, salt, and pepper in a bowl.
    2. Coat the chicken with the marinade and refrigerate for at least 2 hours.
    3. Preheat the grill and cook the chicken for 6-7 minutes on each side.
    4. Serve with a side of grilled vegetables or rice.

Spicy Shrimp Tacos with Lime Crema

- Ingredients:

    1. 1 lb shrimp, peeled and deveined
    2. 1 tbsp chili powder
    3. 1 tsp cumin
    4. 1 tbsp lime juice
    5. 1/2 cup sour cream
    6. 1 tbsp mayonnaise
    7. 1 tbsp lime zest
    8. Warm tortillas

- Instructions:

    1. Toss the shrimp with chili powder, cumin, and lime juice.
    2. Heat a pan over medium heat and cook the shrimp for 2-3 minutes on each side.
    3. Mix sour cream, mayonnaise, and lime zest to make the crema.
    4. Serve shrimp in tortillas and drizzle with lime crema.

Hot and Sour Soup

- Ingredients:

    1. 4 cups chicken broth
    2. 1/4 cup rice vinegar
    3. 2 tbsp soy sauce
    4. 1 tbsp chili paste
    5. 1/2 cup mushrooms, sliced
    6. 1/4 cup bamboo shoots, sliced
    7. 1 egg, beaten
    8. 1 tsp sesame oil

- Instructions:

    1. Bring chicken broth, vinegar, soy sauce, and chili paste to a boil in a pot.
    2. Add mushrooms and bamboo shoots, cooking for 5 minutes.
    3. Stir in the beaten egg, allowing it to cook in ribbons.
    4. Drizzle with sesame oil and serve hot.

Ghost Pepper Chicken Wings

- Ingredients:

    1. 10 chicken wings
    2. 2 tbsp ghost pepper sauce
    3. 1 tbsp olive oil
    4. 1 tsp smoked paprika
    5. 1/2 tsp garlic powder
    6. 1 tbsp lime juice
    7. Salt to taste

- Instructions:

    1. Preheat the oven to 400°F (200°C).
    2. Toss the chicken wings with olive oil, ghost pepper sauce, paprika, garlic powder, lime juice, and salt.
    3. Place the wings on a baking sheet and bake for 25-30 minutes, flipping halfway through, until crispy and cooked through.
    4. Serve with cooling ranch or blue cheese dip.

Blackened Fish Tacos

- Ingredients:

    1. 4 fish fillets (such as tilapia or cod)
    2. 2 tbsp blackened seasoning
    3. 1 tbsp olive oil
    4. 1/2 cup cabbage, shredded
    5. 1/4 cup sour cream
    6. 1 tbsp lime juice
    7. Warm tortillas

- Instructions:

    1. Coat the fish fillets with blackened seasoning.
    2. Heat olive oil in a skillet over medium-high heat and cook the fish for 3-4 minutes per side until blackened and cooked through.
    3. Mix sour cream and lime juice to make a creamy sauce.
    4. Serve the fish in tortillas with shredded cabbage and a drizzle of lime crema.

Spicy Chorizo Stuffed Peppers

- Ingredients:

    1. 4 bell peppers, halved and seeded
    2. 1 lb chorizo sausage
    3. 1/2 cup cooked rice
    4. 1/2 cup shredded cheese
    5. 1 tbsp cumin
    6. 1/2 tsp chili flakes
    7. Salt and pepper to taste

- Instructions:

    1. Preheat the oven to 375°F (190°C).
    2. Brown the chorizo in a skillet over medium heat. Add cumin, chili flakes, rice, salt, and pepper.
    3. Stuff the peppers with the chorizo mixture and place them in a baking dish.
    4. Top with shredded cheese and bake for 20-25 minutes until the peppers are tender and the cheese is melted.

Firecracker Shrimp

- Ingredients:

    1. 1 lb shrimp, peeled and deveined
    2. 2 tbsp sriracha sauce
    3. 2 tbsp honey
    4. 1 tbsp soy sauce
    5. 1 tbsp lime juice
    6. 1 tbsp sesame oil
    7. 2 tbsp green onions, chopped

- Instructions:

    1. In a bowl, mix sriracha, honey, soy sauce, lime juice, and sesame oil.
    2. Toss the shrimp in the sauce mixture and marinate for 15-20 minutes.
    3. Heat a skillet over medium-high heat and cook the shrimp for 2-3 minutes per side until pink and cooked through.
    4. Garnish with green onions and serve.

Tandoori Chicken

- Ingredients:

    1. 4 chicken thighs
    2. 1/2 cup plain yogurt
    3. 1 tbsp tandoori masala
    4. 1 tbsp lemon juice
    5. 1 tsp turmeric
    6. 1 tsp cumin
    7. 1 tsp coriander
    8. Salt to taste

- Instructions:

    1. Mix yogurt, tandoori masala, lemon juice, turmeric, cumin, coriander, and salt in a bowl.
    2. Coat the chicken thighs in the marinade and refrigerate for at least 2 hours.
    3. Preheat the grill to medium heat and cook the chicken for 5-7 minutes per side until fully cooked.
    4. Serve with naan and cucumber raita.

Spicy Beef Empanadas

- Ingredients:

    1. 1 lb ground beef
    2. 1/2 onion, chopped
    3. 1 tbsp chili powder
    4. 1 tsp cumin
    5. 1/4 tsp cayenne pepper
    6. 1/2 cup green olives, chopped
    7. 1 package empanada dough discs
    8. 1 egg, beaten

- Instructions:

    1. Brown the ground beef with chopped onion in a skillet. Add chili powder, cumin, cayenne pepper, and olives. Cook until the beef is fully cooked.
    2. Place a spoonful of the beef mixture onto each empanada disc and fold to seal.
    3. Brush the tops with beaten egg and bake at 375°F (190°C) for 20-25 minutes until golden brown.

Spicy Lamb Koftas

- Ingredients:

    1. 1 lb ground lamb
    2. 1/2 onion, grated
    3. 2 cloves garlic, minced
    4. 1 tbsp cumin
    5. 1 tsp coriander
    6. 1 tsp paprika
    7. 1/2 tsp cayenne pepper
    8. 1 tbsp fresh parsley, chopped
    9. Salt and pepper to taste

- Instructions:

    1. Mix ground lamb, onion, garlic, cumin, coriander, paprika, cayenne, parsley, salt, and pepper in a bowl.
    2. Form the mixture into small meatballs or oblong koftas.
    3. Grill or cook in a skillet over medium heat for 5-7 minutes per side until cooked through.
    4. Serve with pita bread and tzatziki sauce.

Harissa Chicken Thighs

- Ingredients:

    1. 4 chicken thighs
    2. 2 tbsp harissa paste
    3. 1 tbsp olive oil
    4. 1 tbsp lemon juice
    5. 1/2 tsp cumin
    6. Salt and pepper to taste

- Instructions:

    1. Mix harissa paste, olive oil, lemon juice, cumin, salt, and pepper in a bowl.
    2. Coat the chicken thighs with the marinade and let it sit for at least 1 hour.
    3. Preheat the grill to medium-high heat and cook the chicken for 6-7 minutes per side until fully cooked.
    4. Serve with couscous or roasted vegetables.

Sweet and Spicy Korean Fried Chicken

- Ingredients:

    1. 10 chicken wings
    2. 1/2 cup cornstarch
    3. 1/2 cup flour
    4. 1 tsp garlic powder
    5. 1/2 tsp paprika
    6. 1/2 tsp cayenne pepper
    7. 1/4 cup gochujang (Korean chili paste)
    8. 2 tbsp honey
    9. 2 tbsp soy sauce
    10. 1 tbsp rice vinegar
    11. 1 tbsp sesame oil

- Instructions:

    1. Mix cornstarch, flour, garlic powder, paprika, cayenne, salt, and pepper. Dredge the chicken wings in the flour mixture.
    2. Heat oil in a deep fryer or large pot and fry the chicken wings for 8-10 minutes until golden brown and crispy.
    3. In a small bowl, combine gochujang, honey, soy sauce, rice vinegar, and sesame oil. Toss the fried wings in the sauce.
    4. Serve with sesame seeds and green onions.

Mango Habanero Pork Tenderloin

- Ingredients:

    1. 1 pork tenderloin
    2. 2 tbsp mango chutney
    3. 1 habanero pepper, minced
    4. 1 tbsp lime juice
    5. 1 tbsp olive oil
    6. Salt and pepper to taste

- Instructions:

    1. Preheat the oven to 375°F (190°C).
    2. Mix mango chutney, habanero pepper, lime juice, olive oil, salt, and pepper in a bowl.
    3. Coat the pork tenderloin with the marinade and roast for 25-30 minutes until the pork reaches an internal temperature of 145°F (63°C).
    4. Slice and serve with rice or roasted vegetables.

Sichuan Spicy Noodles

- Ingredients:

    1. 8 oz noodles
    2. 2 tbsp Sichuan peppercorns
    3. 1 tbsp chili paste
    4. 2 tbsp soy sauce
    5. 1 tbsp rice vinegar
    6. 1 tsp sugar
    7. 1 tbsp garlic, minced
    8. 1 tbsp ginger, minced
    9. 2 green onions, chopped

- Instructions:

    1. Cook the noodles according to the package directions.
    2. In a pan, toast the Sichuan peppercorns over medium heat until fragrant.
    3. In a bowl, mix chili paste, soy sauce, rice vinegar, sugar, garlic, and ginger.
    4. Toss the noodles in the sauce, then sprinkle with toasted peppercorns and green onions.
    5. Serve with additional chili oil if desired.

Chili Garlic Shrimp

- Ingredients:

    1. 1 lb shrimp, peeled and deveined
    2. 2 tbsp chili garlic sauce
    3. 1 tbsp soy sauce
    4. 1 tbsp lime juice
    5. 2 cloves garlic, minced
    6. 1 tbsp olive oil
    7. 1/4 tsp red pepper flakes
    8. Salt and pepper to taste

- Instructions:

    1. Heat olive oil in a skillet over medium-high heat.
    2. Add garlic and sauté until fragrant, about 1 minute.
    3. Add shrimp, chili garlic sauce, soy sauce, lime juice, red pepper flakes, salt, and pepper.
    4. Cook for 3-4 minutes until the shrimp are pink and cooked through.
    5. Serve with rice or pasta.

Cajun Crawfish Etouffee

- Ingredients:

    1. 1 lb crawfish tails
    2. 1/4 cup butter
    3. 1/4 cup flour
    4. 1/2 onion, chopped
    5. 1 bell pepper, chopped
    6. 2 celery stalks, chopped
    7. 2 cloves garlic, minced
    8. 1 cup chicken broth
    9. 1 tbsp Cajun seasoning
    10. 1/2 tsp paprika
    11. 1/4 tsp cayenne pepper
    12. Salt and pepper to taste

- Instructions:

    1. Melt butter in a large skillet over medium heat, then whisk in flour to make a roux. Cook until golden brown.
    2. Add onion, bell pepper, celery, and garlic and sauté until softened.
    3. Add chicken broth, Cajun seasoning, paprika, cayenne, salt, and pepper. Simmer for 10 minutes.

4. Stir in crawfish and cook for 3-4 minutes.

5. Serve over rice.

Peri-Peri Prawns

- Ingredients:

    1. 1 lb prawns, peeled and deveined
    2. 2 tbsp peri-peri sauce
    3. 1 tbsp olive oil
    4. 1 tsp paprika
    5. 1/2 tsp garlic powder
    6. 1 tbsp lemon juice
    7. Salt to taste

- Instructions:

    1. In a bowl, mix peri-peri sauce, olive oil, paprika, garlic powder, lemon juice, and salt.
    2. Toss the prawns in the marinade and refrigerate for 30 minutes.
    3. Heat a skillet over medium-high heat and cook prawns for 2-3 minutes per side until pink and cooked through.
    4. Serve with a side of salad or rice.

Spicy Pork Bulgogi

- Ingredients:

    1. 1 lb ground pork
    2. 2 tbsp gochujang (Korean chili paste)
    3. 1 tbsp soy sauce
    4. 1 tbsp sesame oil
    5. 1 tbsp honey
    6. 2 cloves garlic, minced
    7. 1 tsp ginger, minced
    8. 2 green onions, chopped
    9. 1 tbsp sesame seeds

- Instructions:

    1. In a bowl, mix gochujang, soy sauce, sesame oil, honey, garlic, and ginger.
    2. Add ground pork to the marinade and mix well.
    3. Heat a skillet over medium-high heat and cook the pork for 5-7 minutes, breaking it up into crumbles.
    4. Garnish with green onions and sesame seeds, then serve over rice.

Chili Lime Grilled Steak

- Ingredients:

    1. 2 steaks (your choice of cut)
    2. 1 tbsp chili powder
    3. 1 tsp cumin
    4. 1 tsp paprika
    5. 1 tbsp lime juice
    6. 1 tbsp olive oil
    7. Salt and pepper to taste

- Instructions:

    1. Preheat the grill to medium-high heat.
    2. Mix chili powder, cumin, paprika, lime juice, olive oil, salt, and pepper.
    3. Coat the steaks in the spice mixture.
    4. Grill steaks for 4-5 minutes per side for medium-rare or longer to desired doneness.
    5. Serve with a side of grilled vegetables.

Thai Basil Beef

- Ingredients:
    1. 1 lb ground beef
    2. 2 tbsp soy sauce
    3. 1 tbsp fish sauce
    4. 2 cloves garlic, minced
    5. 1/2 cup Thai basil leaves, chopped
    6. 1 tbsp lime juice
    7. 1 tbsp sugar
    8. 1-2 Thai chilies, minced
    9. 1 tbsp vegetable oil
- Instructions:
    1. Heat vegetable oil in a skillet over medium-high heat.
    2. Add garlic and Thai chilies and sauté until fragrant.
    3. Add ground beef and cook until browned.
    4. Stir in soy sauce, fish sauce, lime juice, sugar, and Thai basil.
    5. Serve with rice.

Baked Buffalo Cauliflower Wings

- Ingredients:
    1. 1 head of cauliflower, cut into florets
    2. 1/2 cup flour
    3. 1/2 cup water
    4. 1 tsp garlic powder
    5. 1 tsp paprika
    6. 1/4 tsp cayenne pepper
    7. 1/2 cup buffalo sauce
    8. 1 tbsp olive oil

- Instructions:
    1. Preheat the oven to 400°F (200°C).
    2. In a bowl, mix flour, water, garlic powder, paprika, cayenne, salt, and pepper to make a batter.
    3. Dip cauliflower florets in the batter, then place them on a baking sheet.
    4. Bake for 25-30 minutes until crispy.
    5. Toss baked cauliflower in buffalo sauce and serve with blue cheese dip.

Fiery Chipotle Mac and Cheese

- Ingredients:

    1. 1 lb elbow macaroni
    2. 2 tbsp butter
    3. 2 tbsp flour
    4. 2 cups milk
    5. 1 cup shredded cheddar cheese
    6. 1/4 cup chipotle sauce
    7. 1 tsp garlic powder
    8. Salt and pepper to taste

- Instructions:

    1. Cook the macaroni according to package directions.
    2. In a saucepan, melt butter and whisk in flour to make a roux.
    3. Slowly add milk, whisking until thickened.
    4. Stir in cheddar cheese, chipotle sauce, garlic powder, salt, and pepper.
    5. Toss the macaroni in the cheese sauce and serve.

Spicy Stuffed Chicken Breast

- Ingredients:

    1. 4 chicken breasts
    2. 1/2 cup cream cheese, softened
    3. 2 tbsp jalapeños, diced
    4. 1 tbsp chili powder
    5. 1/2 tsp cumin
    6. 1/4 tsp cayenne pepper
    7. 1 cup shredded cheddar cheese
    8. Salt and pepper to taste

- Instructions:

    1. Preheat the oven to 375°F (190°C).
    2. In a bowl, mix cream cheese, jalapeños, chili powder, cumin, cayenne, cheddar cheese, salt, and pepper.
    3. Cut a pocket in each chicken breast and stuff with the cream cheese mixture.
    4. Secure with toothpicks and bake for 25-30 minutes until cooked through.
    5. Serve with a side of vegetables.

Sizzling Beef Stir Fry

- Ingredients:

    1. 1 lb beef (flank steak or sirloin), thinly sliced
    2. 2 tbsp soy sauce
    3. 1 tbsp oyster sauce
    4. 1 tbsp sesame oil
    5. 1 tbsp garlic, minced
    6. 1 bell pepper, sliced
    7. 1 onion, sliced
    8. 2 green onions, chopped
    9. 1/2 tsp chili flakes
    10. 1 tbsp vegetable oil

- Instructions:

    1. Heat vegetable oil in a large skillet or wok over medium-high heat.
    2. Add beef and stir-fry for 3-4 minutes until browned.
    3. Add garlic, onion, and bell pepper, stir-fry for another 2-3 minutes.
    4. Stir in soy sauce, oyster sauce, sesame oil, chili flakes, and green onions.
    5. Serve hot with steamed rice.

Korean Spicy Pork Belly

- Ingredients:

    1. 1 lb pork belly, sliced
    2. 2 tbsp gochujang (Korean chili paste)
    3. 1 tbsp soy sauce
    4. 1 tbsp sesame oil
    5. 2 cloves garlic, minced
    6. 1 tbsp ginger, minced
    7. 1 tbsp brown sugar
    8. 2 green onions, chopped
    9. 1 tsp sesame seeds

- Instructions:

    1. In a bowl, combine gochujang, soy sauce, sesame oil, garlic, ginger, and brown sugar.
    2. Marinate the pork belly in the mixture for at least 30 minutes.
    3. Heat a pan over medium-high heat and cook the pork belly for 5-7 minutes until crispy.
    4. Garnish with green onions and sesame seeds.
    5. Serve with rice or lettuce wraps.

Sweet and Spicy Hot Wings

- Ingredients:

    1. 12 chicken wings
    2. 1/4 cup honey
    3. 2 tbsp hot sauce
    4. 1 tbsp soy sauce
    5. 1 tbsp sriracha sauce
    6. 1 tsp garlic powder
    7. 1 tsp paprika
    8. Salt to taste

- Instructions:

    1. Preheat the oven to 400°F (200°C).
    2. In a bowl, mix honey, hot sauce, soy sauce, sriracha, garlic powder, paprika, and salt.
    3. Toss chicken wings in the sauce mixture and place them on a baking sheet.
    4. Bake for 25-30 minutes, flipping halfway through.
    5. Serve hot with ranch or blue cheese dip.

Spicy Indian Butter Chicken

- Ingredients:

    1. 1 lb chicken breast, diced
    2. 1/4 cup butter
    3. 1/2 onion, chopped
    4. 2 cloves garlic, minced
    5. 1 tbsp ginger, minced
    6. 1 tbsp garam masala
    7. 1/2 tsp turmeric
    8. 1/2 tsp cumin
    9. 1/2 cup tomato puree
    10. 1/2 cup heavy cream
    11. 1/2 tsp chili powder
    12. Salt to taste

- Instructions:

    1. Melt butter in a pan over medium heat.
    2. Add onions, garlic, and ginger, cooking until softened.
    3. Stir in garam masala, turmeric, cumin, and chili powder.
    4. Add chicken and cook until browned.

5. Stir in tomato puree and cream, simmer for 15 minutes.

6. Serve with naan or rice.

Chipotle Black Bean Tacos

- Ingredients:

    1. 1 can black beans, drained and rinsed
    2. 1 tbsp chipotle sauce
    3. 1 tbsp lime juice
    4. 1/2 tsp cumin
    5. 1/2 tsp paprika
    6. 8 small corn tortillas
    7. 1/2 avocado, sliced
    8. 1/4 cup cilantro, chopped
    9. Salt to taste

- Instructions:

    1. In a pan, heat black beans with chipotle sauce, lime juice, cumin, paprika, and salt.
    2. Warm tortillas in a separate pan or microwave.
    3. Assemble tacos with beans, avocado, and cilantro.
    4. Serve with a squeeze of lime.

Fire-Grilled Sriracha Steak

- Ingredients:

    1. 2 steaks (your choice of cut)
    2. 2 tbsp sriracha sauce
    3. 1 tbsp soy sauce
    4. 1 tbsp olive oil
    5. 1 tbsp garlic, minced
    6. 1 tbsp honey
    7. Salt and pepper to taste

- Instructions:

    1. Preheat the grill to medium-high heat.
    2. In a bowl, mix sriracha, soy sauce, olive oil, garlic, honey, salt, and pepper.
    3. Coat the steaks in the marinade and let sit for 10-15 minutes.
    4. Grill steaks for 4-5 minutes per side for medium-rare or longer to desired doneness.
    5. Serve with grilled vegetables.

Sizzling Shrimp and Vegetables

- Ingredients:
    1. 1 lb shrimp, peeled and deveined
    2. 1 bell pepper, sliced
    3. 1 zucchini, sliced
    4. 1 onion, sliced
    5. 2 tbsp soy sauce
    6. 1 tbsp olive oil
    7. 2 cloves garlic, minced
    8. 1/2 tsp chili flakes
    9. Salt and pepper to taste

- Instructions:
    1. Heat olive oil in a large skillet over medium-high heat.
    2. Add garlic and sauté for 1 minute.
    3. Add shrimp and cook for 2-3 minutes until pink.
    4. Add bell pepper, zucchini, onion, soy sauce, chili flakes, salt, and pepper.
    5. Stir-fry for another 3-4 minutes until vegetables are tender.

Spicy Korean Kimchi Pancakes

- Ingredients:

    1. 1 cup kimchi, chopped
    2. 1/2 cup all-purpose flour
    3. 1/4 cup water
    4. 1 egg
    5. 1 tbsp gochujang (Korean chili paste)
    6. 1/4 cup green onions, chopped
    7. 1 tbsp sesame oil
    8. Salt to taste

- Instructions:

    1. In a bowl, combine flour, water, egg, gochujang, and a pinch of salt.
    2. Stir in chopped kimchi and green onions.
    3. Heat sesame oil in a pan over medium-high heat.
    4. Pour batter into the pan and cook for 3-4 minutes per side until crispy.
    5. Serve with soy sauce or a dipping sauce.

Spicy Cajun Pasta

- Ingredients:
    1. 8 oz pasta
    2. 1 lb chicken breast, diced
    3. 1 tbsp Cajun seasoning
    4. 2 tbsp olive oil
    5. 1 bell pepper, chopped
    6. 1 onion, chopped
    7. 2 cloves garlic, minced
    8. 1 cup heavy cream
    9. 1/2 cup Parmesan cheese, grated
    10. Salt and pepper to taste
- Instructions:
    1. Cook pasta according to package directions.
    2. In a pan, heat olive oil and cook chicken with Cajun seasoning for 5-7 minutes.
    3. Add bell pepper, onion, and garlic, cooking until softened.
    4. Stir in heavy cream and Parmesan, simmering for 3 minutes.
    5. Toss pasta in the sauce and serve.

Spicy Cilantro Lime Chicken

- Ingredients:

    1. 4 chicken breasts
    2. 2 tbsp cilantro, chopped
    3. 1 tbsp lime juice
    4. 1 tbsp olive oil
    5. 1 tsp chili powder
    6. 1/2 tsp cumin
    7. Salt and pepper to taste

- Instructions:

    1. Preheat grill or skillet to medium-high heat.
    2. In a bowl, mix cilantro, lime juice, olive oil, chili powder, cumin, salt, and pepper.
    3. Coat chicken breasts in the marinade and grill for 6-7 minutes per side.
    4. Serve with rice or a fresh salad.

Fiery Garlic Chili Chicken

- Ingredients:

    1. 4 chicken thighs, boneless and skinless
    2. 1 tbsp chili paste
    3. 2 tbsp soy sauce
    4. 2 tbsp honey
    5. 2 cloves garlic, minced
    6. 1 tbsp sesame oil
    7. 1/2 tsp red pepper flakes
    8. Salt to taste

- Instructions:

    1. In a bowl, combine chili paste, soy sauce, honey, garlic, sesame oil, red pepper flakes, and salt.
    2. Marinate the chicken in the sauce for at least 30 minutes.
    3. Cook chicken in a skillet over medium heat for 6-7 minutes per side until cooked through.
    4. Serve with steamed vegetables or rice.

Chili Mango Fish Tacos

- Ingredients:

    1. 1 lb white fish fillets (cod, tilapia, or mahi-mahi)
    2. 1 tbsp chili powder
    3. 1 tbsp lime juice
    4. 1 mango, diced
    5. 1/2 red onion, diced
    6. 1/4 cup cilantro, chopped
    7. 8 small tortillas
    8. Salt and pepper to taste

- Instructions:

    1. Season fish fillets with chili powder, lime juice, salt, and pepper.
    2. Cook fish on a grill or skillet for 4-5 minutes per side until flaky.
    3. Combine mango, red onion, cilantro, and a squeeze of lime juice in a bowl.
    4. Assemble tacos with fish and mango salsa in tortillas.
    5. Serve with extra lime wedges.

Hot Pepper Jack Grilled Cheese

- Ingredients:

    1. 2 slices bread
    2. 2 slices pepper jack cheese
    3. 1 tbsp butter
    4. 1 tbsp pickled jalapeños, sliced
    5. 1 tbsp mayonnaise

- Instructions:

    1. Spread mayonnaise on one side of each slice of bread.
    2. Place cheese and jalapeños between the slices of bread, mayo side out.
    3. Heat butter in a pan over medium heat and grill the sandwich for 3-4 minutes per side until golden brown.
    4. Serve with a side of tomato soup or chips.

Roasted Jalapeño Popper Chicken

- Ingredients:

    1. 4 chicken breasts
    2. 4 oz cream cheese, softened
    3. 1/4 cup shredded cheddar cheese
    4. 2 tbsp pickled jalapeños, chopped
    5. 1/2 cup breadcrumbs
    6. 1 tbsp olive oil
    7. Salt and pepper to taste

- Instructions:

    1. Preheat oven to 375°F (190°C).
    2. Mix cream cheese, cheddar, and chopped jalapeños in a bowl.
    3. Season chicken breasts with salt and pepper, then stuff with cheese mixture.
    4. Coat the chicken in breadcrumbs and place on a baking sheet.
    5. Drizzle olive oil over the top and bake for 25-30 minutes, until the chicken is cooked through.
    6. Serve with rice or a salad.

Sriracha Honey Grilled Salmon

- Ingredients:

    1. 4 salmon fillets
    2. 2 tbsp sriracha sauce
    3. 2 tbsp honey
    4. 1 tbsp soy sauce
    5. 1 tbsp lime juice
    6. Salt and pepper to taste

- Instructions:

    1. In a bowl, mix sriracha, honey, soy sauce, lime juice, salt, and pepper.
    2. Marinate salmon fillets in the mixture for at least 30 minutes.
    3. Preheat grill to medium-high heat and cook the salmon for 4-5 minutes per side.
    4. Serve with steamed vegetables or rice.

Spicy Tofu Stir Fry

- Ingredients:

    1. 1 block firm tofu, cubed
    2. 1 tbsp soy sauce
    3. 1 tbsp sriracha sauce
    4. 1 tbsp sesame oil
    5. 1 bell pepper, sliced
    6. 1 zucchini, sliced
    7. 2 cloves garlic, minced
    8. 1 tbsp ginger, minced
    9. 2 green onions, chopped
    10. 1 tbsp sesame seeds

- Instructions:

    1. Press tofu to remove excess moisture, then cube it.
    2. Heat sesame oil in a pan over medium-high heat and cook tofu until golden, 5-7 minutes.
    3. Add garlic, ginger, bell pepper, and zucchini, stir-fry for 3-4 minutes.
    4. Stir in soy sauce and sriracha, cooking for another 2 minutes.
    5. Garnish with green onions and sesame seeds.
    6. Serve over rice.

Spicy Marinated Lamb Chops

- Ingredients:
    1. 8 lamb chops
    2. 1 tbsp olive oil
    3. 2 tbsp lemon juice
    4. 2 tbsp garlic, minced
    5. 1 tbsp cumin
    6. 1 tsp chili powder
    7. 1 tsp paprika
    8. 1 tbsp fresh rosemary, chopped
    9. Salt and pepper to taste
- Instructions:
    1. In a bowl, combine olive oil, lemon juice, garlic, cumin, chili powder, paprika, rosemary, salt, and pepper.
    2. Marinate the lamb chops for at least 1 hour.
    3. Preheat grill to medium-high heat.
    4. Grill lamb chops for 4-5 minutes per side for medium-rare.
    5. Serve with roasted potatoes or a side salad.

Fire-Roasted Salsa and Grilled Chicken

- Ingredients:

    1. 4 chicken breasts
    2. 4 tomatoes, halved
    3. 2 jalapeños, halved
    4. 1/2 red onion, quartered
    5. 2 cloves garlic, peeled
    6. 1/4 cup cilantro, chopped
    7. 1 tbsp lime juice
    8. 1 tbsp olive oil
    9. Salt and pepper to taste

- Instructions:

    1. Preheat grill to medium-high heat.
    2. Grill tomatoes, jalapeños, onion, and garlic for 4-5 minutes until charred.
    3. Blend the grilled veggies with cilantro, lime juice, salt, and pepper to make salsa.
    4. Season chicken breasts with olive oil, salt, and pepper, and grill for 5-6 minutes per side.
    5. Serve chicken with fresh salsa on top.

Thai Green Curry with Vegetables

- Ingredients:

    1. 1 can coconut milk
    2. 2 tbsp green curry paste
    3. 1 tbsp soy sauce
    4. 1 tbsp lime juice
    5. 1 bell pepper, sliced
    6. 1 zucchini, sliced
    7. 1/2 cup peas
    8. 1/2 cup carrots, sliced
    9. 1 tbsp fresh basil, chopped
    10. 1 tbsp vegetable oil

- Instructions:

    1. Heat vegetable oil in a pot over medium heat, then stir in green curry paste.
    2. Add coconut milk, soy sauce, and lime juice, simmer for 10 minutes.
    3. Add bell pepper, zucchini, peas, and carrots, cook until tender, about 5 minutes.
    4. Stir in fresh basil and serve with steamed rice.

Spicy Chipotle Salmon

- Ingredients:

    1. 4 salmon fillets
    2. 2 tbsp chipotle sauce
    3. 1 tbsp olive oil
    4. 1 tbsp lime juice
    5. 1/2 tsp garlic powder
    6. Salt and pepper to taste

- Instructions:

    1. Preheat grill or skillet to medium-high heat.
    2. Mix chipotle sauce, olive oil, lime juice, garlic powder, salt, and pepper.
    3. Coat the salmon fillets in the marinade and let sit for 10 minutes.
    4. Grill or cook salmon for 4-5 minutes per side.
    5. Serve with a side of quinoa or sautéed vegetables.

www.ingramcontent.com/pod-product-compliance
Lightning Source LLC
LaVergne TN
LVHW081322060526
838201LV00055B/2413